KENDALL SHAREEF

THIS BOY'S A LION

Contents

II   The Wild Heart

III   The Family

I

The Journey

How We Got Here

9 Months

One day,
    mother and father had a good time.
    K-i-s-s-i-n-g.
    One thing lead to another,
    and inside mama's belly
    was a baby me.

Nameless at the moment,
    and I took on a different form,
    a different shape,
    then mama gained the power to shapeshift,
    and then she donned her cape.

And although she was filled with mixed emotions,
    she still carried me
    in every sense of the word.
    And even though she questioned herself,
    she still had hopes
    that I'd fly higher than the average bird.

Meanwhile,
    father was busy dealing with things

feeling out of his control,
but he tried
and tried his best
to ease my mother's soul.
Then he searched and searched
for answers
about how to best fulfill
his fatherly role.
And I just know
all that heavy thinking
had to take its toll.

Then many months later,
life was the game that I was ready to play,
the day we are born,
what a beautiful,
wonderful day.

Birthday

It's an August night,
   and I couldn't wait to see
   mother and father in person.

I couldn't wait to arrive.
   And I was ready to pop out quick,
   so uncle had to drive.
   Rise in power Charles Canada,
   I still remember when
   you were alive,

you sped to the hospital
   so mama could get inside.
   Bump on her belly,
   call it a bumpy ride.

Dad got the news,
   so in his car he flied.
   He had to see this moment,
   I was his joy,
   I was his pride.

Then mama
    got to the hospital,
    on the gurney she lied,
    no time for painkillers
    so I bet that she cried,
    but she pushed
    and she pushed,
    and for the first time
    I got to see the world outside.

Greetings from the other side,
    I'm the young boy
    that my father named Kendall.

And joy filled the room
    as my life's song
    hit it's big crescendo,

then love struck mom
    and threw all her pain
    out the window.

I don't even remember this day,
    but I sure can pretend though.

I can't believe I could
    forget that special night
    in 1994,
    sigh,
    ah well,
    time to explore.

Crawl

On the ground
  is not where I'll stay.
  But it's the place
  where I begin.

Even the slightest movement
  forward
  is some type of,
  kind of,
  win.

At the moment
  this is all I know,
  so on my face I have a grin.

Crawling, sprawling,
  on the floor,
  building up
  the strength within.

Forward is where I'm going,
  and back there

is where I've been.

Walk

From the ground I rise,
  and my feet touch the earth.

It's a whole new world,
  and I've experienced
  some type of rebirth.

My potential seemed bottomless,
  as it expanded
  and increased its girth.

And my feet were now priceless to me,
  far more than gold is worth.
  What a funny thought
  I would think
  as I went on to express much mirth.

Run

Gotta move fast,
   I can't sit still,
   I have somewhere I have to be.

I can hear it all so well,
   it's so loud,
   something is calling me.

It's begging me to dip
   a toe in,
   then dive into
   my own personal sea.

It says if you come
   running here
   then you're bound to feel free.

Bound to feel free?
   How can I be bound and free
   I ask,
   it says no,
   I mean

you're bound to
  leap over any false reality.

So I collect my dignity
  then take both my eyes
  and see,

that it wasn't a lie after all.

The water is glowin ,
  the waves are calm,
  and the way
  that it's flowin,

is music to my
  left and right ear,
  now I'm sprinting,
  and I'm dashing,
  so keep my lane clear.

Fly

I reach my own
   personal sea,
   and none of it was a lie.
   The moment I took one leap,
   wings sprouted,
   and I was in the sky.

Stretch my wings a little bit,
   and I begin to fly.

Soaring now above a cloud,
   a ray of sun gets in my eye.

Birds chirp chirping,
   as they went flying by.

Then poof,
   my wings disappeared,
   and something went awry.

Landing

I remember I cried the first day I went to private school.
   I was looking for mom and dad
   in a sea of unfamiliar faces.

There's a picture in a photo album
   to prove that this part isn't a lie.

Though, sometime from now
   I would learn to fabricate the truth.
   But it was at this same school
   that I lost my first tooth.

There're witnesses,
   so remember this part isn't a lie.

At this same private school,
   I liked to ask questions
   and my favorite word was why.

And the teacher could only ask
   why I wasn't quiet like my brother.
   Don't believe me?

Go ask my mother.

She'll tell you it's facts.
    She'll tell you
    she defended my honor,
    while the teacher wished
    that I would fit in.

But I was only 5,
    and I wanted to fly,
    so I had no time to pretend.

Tripping

Public school was a bigger challenge.

Although I wasn't yet the king of lies,
   so many made jokes about my feet
   and the way I walk,
   cuz my toes were pigeons
   like the birds that fly through skies.

Many attempted to make jokes,
   and took about a hundred tries.

And when I heard there was a surgery
   to fix this "problem",
   it came as a great surprise.

But was it really
   because of the health of me,
   that I decided to agree,
   or was it just well hidden
   insecurity?

I'm not exactly sure right now,

I'd have to consult with
the third and fourth grade me.

Who am I kidding?
  I know they'd both say
  I was trying to flee,
  they'd say I was desperate
  for a place I could be at peace,
  and just...be.

Stumbling

When I became middle grade,
   the fact that I told lies
   became the truth.

And for every how you doing
   my parents asked,
   I was always fine.

But in actuality,
   the reality was
   that things were
   getting out of line.

I was the topic of many jokes,
   and my appearance
   the punchline.
   People were all up in my business
   as I was just minding mine.

E.T.,
   Alien,
   Peanut head,

I still remember every line.

And I thought,
    what if I could make up a story,
    it'll give them something to talk about,
    a narrative that I control.

But in all honesty,
    all it really did
    was weigh heavy on my soul.

And for every lie
    that I told in search of peace
    and fun,
    oh I wish,
    how I wish,
    that they could be undone.
    But I'll take the blame for all of them,
    and I promise I will not run.

Stagger

The high school me
   forgot the great ocean he was,
   and kept getting hit with waves
   while trapped inside
   a jealous sea.
   He saw the love
   that they all got,
   and couldn't help but think
   that that should be me.

But his uniqueness was his power,
   and that was something
   he had yet to see.

And if I were to ask
   the high school me
   what he wanted to be,
   he'd say a singer,
   playing basketball,
   and probably on tv.

He'd want all the recognition

that came with fame.
He'd want everyone
screaming
and chanting his name.

And he'd want to be inducted
into some kind of
hall of fame.

And high school me
would've loved
a large entourage.
But high school produces
so many chameleons
walking around
in camouflage.

That ever changing skin.

High school me was a dragon,
but shrank into
a tiny lizard,
stretching himself thin.

Ain't it funny how you always end up the outcast
when every move you made was
an attempt to fit in.

Well, it must've never been meant for me.
But that's a lesson
that the high school me

had yet to learn.
At the time he was only concerned
with
how many admirers he could earn.

And when he saw all the admiration
that the athletes got,
he thought
he wanted to take a turn.

So varsity basketball was his aim,
ever since freshman year,
when he was new to things
and his face
was still super clear.
But that was
until all that bumpiness
appeared junior year.

Marks on his face,
that he wish would
disappear.
They called him pizza face and other names,
but he didn't shed a tear.

He just bottled the scream inside,
so nobody could hear.
He was always this silly, goofy
kid,
but being alone was his fear.

Pick Me Up

College came,
   and the bumps on the pavement of my face
   started to smooth over,
   and it seemed like a real good chance for some kind of do-
over.

Freshman year,
   the slate was clean,
   and there weren't too many
   who knew me from before.
   So I decided
   I'd come in with a little swagger,
   as soon as I walked through the door.

But my own emotions
   were often the signals
   that I'd choose to ignore.
   I'd keep watering places I didn't grow in
   even after seeing all the strange fruit that it bore.
   And when I tried to be peaceful with others,
   deep inside me there was war.

And what's more,

I felt wedged between
   a mountain, a society, and a hard place,
   not connecting to any side,
   and when I studied for my sociology degree
   I felt like some of those books had lied.

Cuz when they teach of social norms and society,
   I never see or hear of anything quite like me.

And at times, I didn't even feel like a person,
   so I was the mighty oak
   that only showed the shadow of my tree.

But really, a person is just a persona we wear
   to cloak and shroud ourselves in normalcy,
   but no one's really normal see,

because in reality,
   no two people are alike.
   But society just sets its expectations,
   and expects us to handle the bars it sets for us
   like we were riding on a bike.

I was riding half-heartedly too
   until my soul said sike.
   It grew tired of me doing things
   that I ain't even like.

And with so much of me left to discover,

I found some wilderness in my mind
and decided to take a hike.

New Balance

As I was writing this,
   I realized that I never wanted to fit in,
   I just wanted the peace and freedom to be fully me.
   But the irony with that is,
   I was already born free.

The home where my heart belonged
   was always inside of me.
   Makes sense, don't it?
   Because when you take the heart out of you,
   then life will cease to be.

And in order for me to get free,
   I had to recognize that I was simply treading water,
   next to her, her, and him.
   And I was treading water for a while,
   but I started to swim,
   going from their river to my ocean,
   and losing all sight of them.

Then when I saw a younger me playing in the water,
   I had to say sorry to him.

Told him his shine was so beautiful,
   and I'm sorry I made it go dim,
   he said you live and you learn,
   now will you sink or you swim,
   then I told him to lead the way
   and started following him,
   we started talking about life,
   uncovering gem after gem,
   and the dopest thing he said
   was:
   it doesn't matter how many take shots at ya
   as long as you protect the rim.

And we swam, and we swam, reunited again.

II

The Wild Heart

Scattered Thoughts

Should've. Could've. Would've.

I kept some doors open that I should've taken my hand to slam and close,

but I was allured by any person or experience that took on the appearance of a rose.

And I suppose, it was my attempt at making deep connections, in the most unlikeliest of places, but weak and brittle roots were hidden behind the prettiest of vases.

And in many cases, I should've, could've, would've done something different, looking at it today.

But what's done is done. I can shift and alter the future, but I can't really change yesterday.

Wild Heart

Dress me up in stylish clothes
  to gain the attention of those who do not care.
  Impress her, impress him,
  oh my, the silliness is in the air.

My heart's despair,
  hits my rib cage
  and plays xylophone,
  then it calls my name,
  but the dial tone,
  is too loud,
  and I can't use my senses to the best of their ability.

My wild heart loves the chaos,
  but also loves stability.

Sometimes my heart swims effortlessly in the instability,
  but maybe if I tell it to calm down then it will agree.

Not true.

Because as I reflect, and talk to myself

in the form of a soliloquy,
I realize I'm the peacock all grown up
that the world has taught humility.

But why humble myself
in a world that's so finnicky?
I should be proud to be me,
and not my own worst enemy.
So go on my wild heart,
I've decided to set you free.

Who Is Society?

Who is society?
  Who is they?

Don't ask me, I don't really know.
  Just some people who said life had to be this way, very long
ago.

They say this is how people act,
  then we put on a little show.
  Then we hide behind a persona
  that dims and eclipses our own personal glow.

Then we show fractions of ourselves,
  showing only the acceptable.

Normal

Normal is a wave
  that leaves us drowning,
  it's an emotion
  that leaves hearts frowning.

Normal is where you go to die,
  and something else walks in your shoes.
  Normal is when nobody wins,
  and the whole world starts to lose.

No normal person thought outside the box,
  they stayed stuck inside the boat,
  hoping it never rocks.

Come on in the water's fine,
  even after the boat tips over,
  the water taste great
  and only comes up to your shoulders.

And if it feels like it's a burden to carry yourself,
  I'd compare it to the lightest of boulders,
  cuz as you get older and older,

a lot of things just stop to matter,
you stop caring bout all the chatter,
and it's your own voice that starts to sound the warmest.
So just know, there's no need for you to put on a show
in this world that's so conformist.

You were meant to be bigger than life,
  Elephant style enormous.

Elephant

I burst out the box I put me in,
   now I'm the elephant in the room.
   I grew too big to play so small,
   and now even my slightest movement goes boom
   And this isn't a piece about bragging,
   but I'm sure by now the opposite is what you'd assume.

I guess what I'm trying to say is,
   the fact that we exist makes us incredible.

Take me for example,
   I was such a tiny hopeful seed,
   but I blossomed into a mighty flower.

As I collected energies from the sun,
   I discovered that the Sol was my power.
   So I sat with mine for a minute or two,
   no, it was maybe an hour.
   And As I looked within my heart,
   my mind began to devour,
   things that brought me fear
   and things that once made me cower.

It was then that
    I realized,
    we're all born to make an impact
    like a meteor shower.

So I made things happen
    with the lemons I was given,
    even though the initial taste
    was sour.
    But all the vitamins helped me see
    that we've got so much firepower.

I've got the power,
    and you've got it too,
    and it's nothing to sneeze at
    so we won't hear achoo,
    and we've come so far since we were kids,
    just look how much we grew.

And there's something I gotta tell you one time,
    no, better yet let's make that two:
    any progress is progress when you walk your path,
    just always see it through.
    now go back to that same line again,
    and may you find your power too,
    cuz any progress is progress when you walk your path,
    just always see it through.

Barefoot

I can't fit in these shoes you gave me,
   cuz they're much too small.
   My feet stretch around the earth
   and prop me up to a height that's
   incredibly tall.

Still, I tried so hard to squeeze my feet in,
   but it only caused me aching.
   Then one day I found out how to shrink a foot,
   but in the end my heart was breaking.

So I stretched out my feet once again,
   thrown shoes
   now gone with the wind,
   free to be,
   barefoot, again.

Empathy

They say
    place yourself in their shoes,
    but we all wear a different size,
    and different is the key word
    cuz your uniqueness is a prize,
    and as long as you remain present you're a gift,
    so after the BS
    we rise,
    and if somebody said there ain't nothing special in you,
    well then somebody lies.

There's a multitude of people just waiting to play outside,
    just gotta hop in your own boat,
    catch your own wave,
    then just let that thing ride.

Trust In You

Trust in the you
 that made it through the yesterdays and todays.
 Trust in the you
 that dispelled the skies that were looking filled with greys.

Trust in the you
 that brought sunshine to somebody's rain.
 Trust in the you
 that lived through incredible pain.

Trust in the you
 who made someone laugh,
 someone smile.
 Trust in the you
 you haven't allowed yourself to be in a while.

Trust in the you
 that is as everlasting as a mountain.
 Trust in your hopeful, wishful-self
 like coins in the fountain.

Trust in the you

who holds an incredible truth,
but most of all
trust in you.

You

You were born with all the paints, dyes, and brushes,
   to create a perfect masterpiece,
   as long as you can master peace,
   and not let the world be a thief,
   of your joy,
   young girl, young boy.

For you are of the universe,
   one incredible song,
   born of this world,
   you were meant to belong.

King Of The Hill

I've seen it rain down cruel words from people clouds.
   And the droplets of hate, had wet my clothes,
   leaving me feeling exposed.

Many have tried to hurt my growth,
   like bad tendons near the knee,
   then they told me to come down from way up there,
   just like the ax told the tree.

Next I heard a loud thump,
   but the only one in this forest was me.

And I can attest that,
   even if no one is around,
   it always makes a sound,
   when something that mighty and grand
   slams to the ground.

Trust me, I'd know.

For a while, I just sat there
   impossibly still,

but then I saw a ray of sun
flicker across a hill,
making it to the top of it
took almost all of my skill,
but still,
I willed it so,
then looked to and fro.

What a beauty to behold.

I saw the tree pick itself back up,
as the ground sprouted flowers,
the air whispered excellence
as we both recognized our true powers,
I stood as the king of the hill,
embracing it all for several hours.
Daylight turned into night dark
as darkness devours,
the day is won,
and victory is ours.

Whispers

Earth's whisper told me:
    Keep going,
    almost there said the sky,
    you are my precious shooting star,
    you are more than meets the eye.

The stars whisper:
    Shine bright,
    just like we light the night,
    and take a fire to your passions
    and watch them ignite.

Young Star

Youngster young star,
   don't burn out too soon.

Youngster young star,
   shine brighter than the sun,
   and shoot for well past the moon.

Youngster young star,
   you don't need to be friends with everyone around,
   ironically the things that naturally gravitate towards you
   are the things that won't keep you down.

Note To Self

To the me who knew how to fly,
  I'm sorry I put you on the ground.

And to the young me who was stumbling through things,
  for you, I'll be the best hero around.

And when I think of you,
  I'll no longer be angry at you,
  because you got me through those days.

And I'll always love you no matter what,
  even if you were just a phase

And even if the world don't accept me,
  I'll only ever need your praise.

And I remember we used to fear being singled out,
  but they're gonna talk anyways.

So let's combine every spark and ember of our passionate heart
  and set all our doubts ablaze.

Self Talk

I wrote myself a letter,
   and in it, it said this:
   Dear me,
   I can see confusion knows your name
   as you stare at the abyss.
   I saw you take aim at trying to understand these feelings,
   but sadly, I watched you miss.
   I've seen you tiptoe between the borderline of chaos
   and the perfect state of bliss.
   But deep down, I know you know that something is amiss.

Now can I ask you a question?
   Can I really, Really ask you a question?
   Cuz I feel this is something you oughta know.

What are these feelings that I'm feeling?
   Do they even have a name?
   Cuz I keep feeling all these things at once
   and now my heart thinks it's a game.
   Then my mind gets grip of the wheel
   and starts driving me insane,
   then confusion seeps from neurons

invading every crevice of my brain.

Oops, look at me,
  I've already established that you don't know the answer,
  but I guess the confusion made me ask,
  and it's a bit saddening
  because explaining me to me should be such a simple task,
  but it looks like I'll have to keep pulling and chipping away
  at this old ancient mask,
  until all is revealed
  and in the sunlight I'll bask

Oh, and P.S.
  I apologize for my past actions,
  because back in the day
  I treated you too rough.
  But I love you,
  I love me,
  and we will always be more than enough.
  Love, yourself

P.P.S.
  *Rise in Power Charles Canada, aka Uncle Charles, this was the
  first piece I wrote after hearing the news about you.*

III

The Family

Nothing But Love

Uncle Charles

I still hear your laugh.
   You lived life like you always had an inside joke going on with
yourself,
   as if an invisible comedian was always whispering their best
material into your ears.
   And even though many may say that you are no longer here,
   I still feel you near.

And you've reminded us all that our time here is not forever,
   and it feels as if I'm being reminded to use mine in a way
that's clever,
   and live with no regrets.

Grandma Judy

My love for you is so vast
   that the ocean gets jealous.
   Kindness comes from every inch of you
   and each of our moments I relish.

See, my heart has a special place for you,
   and forever in it you'll exist.
   And if you asked me to write down all the times I loved you,
   I'd be writing a forever endless list.

And if you needed it,
   I'd tell you I love you
   a trillion, billion times
   if that is truly what you wished.

I love you
   I love you
   I love you,

I'm sure you get the gist.

Mother

I first said hello to you in the summer of 1994,
  and ever since then, you'd give me one reason to love you,
  and then you'd give me many reasons more.

And even though my heart and voice can be gentle at times,
  for you, I'd go to war.
  And you could call my love for you the sands by the ocean,
  because it's real and it'll always be shore.

Now let me tell you something I ain't neva told you before,
  a smile runs across my face every time you walk through a
door,
  and I love you today,
  tomorrow,
  and forevermore.

Father

I was going to write something fancy,
    but it appears that my lexicon couldn't quite suffice,
    cuz your existence is indescribable,
    and something I'll never encounter twice.

And my love for you is free of charge,
    it will never come with a price.
    cuz I've loved you forever,
    well forever and a day if we're being precise.
    And to my life you add a unique spice,
    so spending more days with you would surely be nice.

Adonis

From bunk beds to our own rooms, the glo up was real.
  Little brother is all grown up now,
  man, how old does that make me feel?
  Whether we were wildin or the moment was just chill ,
  I hold on to all of those memories still .

And I should tell you that
  you are one of my biggest motivators, and to hear
  you say proudly, "that's my brother,"
  is music to my ears.

And sometimes with the thought of you in mind,
  I've faced down some crazy fears.

And when I hear someone speak well of you,
  in my head I'm like, yeah, I already know.

I love to see you shine,
  and it's been a pleasure to watch you grow.
  And if life began to be defined as tv channels,
  then you'd be one incredible show.

And speaking of shows,
    my love for you will span longer
    than the length of time that Oda decides to let one piece go,
    cuz this love has no expiration date,
    and I just thought that you should know.

I love you little brother.

Rahsaan

To my brother from the same mother,
   I don't really say I love you enough.

The feeling is deep within my heart,
   and it is truly no bluff.

Your happy is my happy,
   I love to see your joy.
   And it almost brings tears to my eyes
   when I see you and your little boy.

And I'm glad to see your smile,
   because I can tell that it's real,
   and I'll say I love you as many times
   as I need to, to get across how I feel.

I love you,
   now times that by infinity.

Jamal

You're always yourself,
   consistently you,
   staying Jamal, the truest of true,
   just know that your nephew is so proud of you.

Proud of your courage to just stay yourself,
   despite the push and the sway from everyone else.

I respect your stick-to-itiveness
   and the way you forge your own path.
   And should anyone ever do you wrong,
   then they shall surely face my wrath.

I see you; I love you,
   and this bond is no fake.
   I'd have to call it covalent
   cuz it'd be difficult to break.

And we won't shake,
   cuz we've been building on solid ground,
   you started as an uncle,
   and in your heart,

a true friend is what I've found.

Grandma Princess

Your love is stronger than a gamma-ray burst.
   The atmosphere changes when I'm around you,
   like I've left planet earth.

And even if I ever had doubts about myself,
   you always showed me that a lot is what I'm worth.

The oceans of your love
   are vaster than the universe.
   You don't push away,
   you pull us in,
   and then we all immerse.

Thank you for loving me
   and for putting us first.

Grandpa Na'eem

I almost always see you kind,
   I always see you as yourself,
   best grandpa I could ask for,
   wouldn't trade you for anyone else.

With understanding and acceptance,
   built upon solid ground,
   you add to the room's energy whenever your around.
   Story after story,
   by now your tales are renowned,
   and surely not to be missed.
   And I don't have to go searching for someone
   who takes the time to care,
   because you already exist.

Marissa

Sing your song,
    sing your song,
    cuz your truth is so beautiful.

Never stop what you do,
    cuz you're always being you-tiful.

And with that light,
    you have what it takes to make
    every mountain moveable.

So sing your song,
    sing your song,
    cuz I love your life,
    the musical.

Tania

You do Tania things in Tania ways,
  so unapologetically you.

And even if all eyes are watching,
  you'd just do more of your thang
  and probably stare back too.

And for that, I have much respect.

And never doubt if I love you,
  cuz I'm sure that I do,
  since I double, triple checked.

Lloryn

When I first met you, I didn't even know we were family.

    You saw the last name on my name tag, then told me we were cousins.

    And ever since then, I always thought that we had to have met for a reason.

I don't quite know what that reason is yet, but as I reflect,
    what I do know is I'll be here for you every season.
    And I know we don't talk as much,
    and we can feel out of touch,
    but this love is something you
    can believe in.
    And whenever life gets odd and stacks the odds against you,
    I'll try to help you find a way to get even.

Auntie Linda

I appreciate you Auntie,
  you're always showing much support.

Ask me to find any time I didn't love you,
  then I'd have no incidents to report,
  cuz I'd be undefeated if loving who you were
  became a sport.

Courtney

I'll be right here,
    always wishing you the best.

I've got an account full of love,
    and in you I shall invest.

And I'll be right there, cheering you on
    as you embark on any quest.

And my love for our family,
    is truly no jest,
    so let my love reach your ears,
    and not go unexpressed.

Cassius

Your uncle loves you,
    you adorable little king.

And if you only learn one lesson from your uncle,
    then I hope it's that you never let anyone stop you from
    doing your thing.

Follow any dream that makes your heart sing,
    and don't worry,
    if you ever forget how to fly,
    then your uncle can always lend you a wing.

Made in the USA
Las Vegas, NV
25 April 2021